Backyard Monarchs

Written by, Ashley Gregory

All photographs taken by, Ashley Gregory

The life cycle of a monarch butterfly is fascinating! From a tiny egg on a milkweed leaf, to a caterpillar, then a chrysalis, and finally a beautiful butterfly.

Monarch caterpillars only eat milkweed plants.

So, monarch butterflies only lay their eggs on milkweed plants.

When a
caterpillar hatches
from the egg,
it is so small!

The caterpillar eats and eats and grows so fast!

These caterpillars grew so much they got too big for their skin.

Look closely and you can see they shed their skin.

Now they can eat and grow even more!

Look for these caterpillars
on the underside of leaves.

Sometimes, they hang
upside down on the stem.

After the monarch caterpillar eats a lot of milkweed, it leaves the plant to search for a place to become a chrysalis.

The caterpillar to the left is crawling along some mulch. The caterpillar above has found a safe place in a nearby palm tree.

Once the monarch caterpillar decides on a safe place to pupate, or transform into a chrysalis, it spins a small pad of silk.

Can you see the white silk pad the caterpillar is making?

The caterpillar hangs from the silk pad in the shape of a J or ⌡ until it sheds its skin one last time.

This caterpillar shed its skin
and became the chrysalis
you see here.

The monarch chrysalis hardens and becomes smooth. It protects the change, or metamorphosis, that is occuring inside.

The chrysalis is green. It has a little bit of gold and black on it as well.

Can you find the chrysalis in each of the photographs?

In 10 - 14 days
the chrysalis
becomes transparent.
You can see the
butterfly inside!

This means the
butterfly is ready to
eclose, or emerge,
from the chrysalis!

After the butterfly emerges from the chrysalis, fluid from its abdomen pumps through its wings. This helps the wings expand and dry so the butterfly can eventually fly away.

This monarch
butterfly is a male
butterfly.

It has thin black
webbing on its
wings.

It also has two black
dots on the hind
wings.

This butterfly has thick black webbing and no black spots.

It is a female butterfly.

If you want to see these beautiful butterflies in your yard try planting milkweed!

Further Reading:

"Monarch Butterfly" by, Jason Cooper

"Monarch Butterfly" by, Gail Gibbons

"The World of the Monarch Butterfly" by, Eric Grace

"Monarch Butterfly Migration" by, Grace Hansen

www.ingramcontent.com/pod-product-compliance
Lightning Source LLC
Chambersburg PA
CBHW040146240726
48664CB00002B/613